The Prayer of
A Modern Man

The Prayer of
A Modern Man

by

Louis Evely

Translated from the French by Noel Rae

DIMENSION BOOKS
Wilkes-Barre, Pennsylvania

1878

Published by Dimension Books

Wilkes-Barre, Pennsylvania

Copyright 1968 by Dimension Books, Inc.

Nihil Obstat: Imprimatur

    Vincent P. Molloy   ✠ Lawrence B. Casey
    Censor Librorum   Bishop of Paterson
    October 9, 1968   October 9, 1968

Library of Congress Catalog Card Number 68-31385

TABLE OF CONTENTS

The Prayer of
A Modern Man

The Prayer of

A Modern Man

When we are confronted with what may be a divine manifestation — a vision, an annunciation, a transfiguration — there are two things that we must always do. First of all we must distrust it, refuse to believe in it right away, but secondly we must hold on to it, scrutinize it closely, mull it over, examine it. When we deal with the things of God we must be as innocent as the dove and as wise as the serpent, but above all keep our common sense. We should never disbelieve, for God is everywhere and nothing is done without God, but we should never believe too quickly either.

Look at the example of the Virgin Mary. She asked questions, thought things over, sought for advice, read the Scriptures, de-

9

manded of the angel a sign. All that took time.

When we are dealing with the Word of God, or with some striking event in the world of faith, there are two foolish ways of behaving. The first is to say, "That's wonderful, terrific, I understand it completely!" And the second is to say, "This is awful, I can't understand it at all!" Somewhere between these two extremes lies the only proper attitude toward every manifestation or Word of God: the attitude of the Virgin Mary. She did not understand what the angel said to her, but she pondered these things, she meditated on them in her heart.

It is important to recognize that *waiting* for God and a certain *readiness* or availability for him will bring things out right in the end.

The light of God is somewhat like a bad fluorescent light. When you go into a room that has such lighting and turn on the switch, what happens? Nothing at all. You have to wait, and in the meantime you can't see a thing. But if you are a bit nervous or irritable or impulsive or impatient, what do you do? You say, "I can't see a thing in here," and you leave the room. Or else you lose your temper and turn the switch off again, and then you can be quite certain that you won't be able to see anything at all. But what should you have done? You should have waited. And then what would you have seen? A few pale flickerings of light in the fluorescent tube, and finally the illumination you wanted.

So read the Scriptures. Ask for advice and listen to it. Keep your eyes and your ears open for things that apply to you and that will help you understand. And what else should you do? Learn to wait!

At a given moment the light will come. It's hard to tell exactly when that moment will arrive, but all of a sudden it comes, and everything turns out right.

You must reflect passively, not actively, for it is precisely those areas that we cannot reach by ourselves that will be illuminated by the light of God.

Learn to let events take their course. Let time and the grace of God do their work. Let the Holy Spirit tell your heart what it is that you need. Don't try to choose for yourself. Keep an open mind and don't get carried away by curiosity. Let things work themselves out. That is the way to understand the Scriptures, indeed life itself.

11

Meditate. Examine your life. Fnd your life in the Scriptures and the Scriptures in your life.

All this forms a theme that is vital to Christian life. Real faith, the faith of an adult, is above all else a faith that is trusting. It is not always necessary that we should understand. Believing is not the same thing as understanding. To believe is to take on trust. It is to have understood enough so that we can accept not understanding for a while, not seeing for a while. It is to have enough light of our own so that we can endure the darkness. It is to remain faithful in the darkness to what we have seen in the light.

Faith is trusting, but faith is also independent. You must not believe just because those around you believe or because of a feeling of loyalty to those who have spoken to you of facts, to the pillars of their churches and the God. Too many people cling to the external cassocks of their priests, and have never gotten any farther. I was recently told the story of a person who got so angry with his local priest, with the liturgy in the vernacular, with the Council and with Pope Paul VI that he refused to be married in a church. He was one of those who cling only to the external facts. If we do that, we will never get anywhere.

What is needed is a faith that is independent of external circumstances. And what is needed is a faith that is committed — totally committed.

By commitment is meant putting faith in our life and life in our faith.

For me the Gospel is committed to life and life to the Gospel. Everything that is true in the Gospel is true in my life. Everything that is true in my life is true in the Gospel. The Gospel is a wonderful light for my life, and my life helps me to understand the Gospel properly.

It is not true to say that extraordinary things happened two thousand years ago that will never happen again. Such things are happening all the time. God still loves. He still suffers. He still restores to life. He still nourishes. He still multiplies his blessings. He still appears. If you don't believe that, then you don't believe anything. He still lives. He still loves. He still heals. He still pardons. He still saves. Our redeemer is alive.

Beware of illusion, and beware also of illumination. It takes time and the help of the Church and of the Scriptures before you can be sure of the truth of your inspirations. But it also takes faith, faith that God is constantly at work and that the evidence of his presence can be found.

Faith. Time. The wisdom of the serpent. The innocence of the dove. None of this is easy.

Let us now apply all this to prayer, and ponder two aspects which are basically the same: prayer as an experience of faith, and prayer as a meeting with God.

What happens in prayer? Why do people pray? When I pray, do I come into contact with someone, or am I deluding myself?

Prayer is above all a place for meeting the Lord. If we don't pray, we cannot know Him. If we don't pray, we don't know who the Lord is.

I believe that it is impossible to be converted without prayer and also that nothing is more sincere than the prayer of an unbeliever. Prayer helps all of us in those areas in which we are unbelievers, and those areas are vast. We are always seeking the truth and never finding it completely. Thus we are all partially unbelievers, even those of us who say we live by faith.

The Church is also seeking. She is holding

Councils, she is saying that even the dogmas that she has already defined could be defined better. For there can be progress in the definition of dogma, in the way of expressing what is revealed, and that is what the Church is trying to do. If you say the same thing twice, the second time you say it, it is less true than the first because truth is a relationship between the person who speaks it and the person who hears it, and these two people will have changed in the interval. And since the two people have changed, if you maintain the same relationship in other respects, what you say has become a little less true. That is why the Church, by repeating herself too often, has ended up by speaking to no one. She even spoke in Latin. . . .

What also destroys the Church is routine among the clergy. Not thinking about what they are doing, not thinking about what they are saying; all of which leads to ignorance among the faithful. Hardly anyone talks to the clergy anymore. There is only a pretense of talking to them. Nothing of any significance is said. Great care is lavished on saying nothing in the Church!

I have just been reading a wonderful book about a priest whose bishop puts him in charge of a local religious newspaper and tells him to write about anything he likes except religious questions, because that would be dangerous. The bishop was a cardinal and was afraid of the Roman Curia, and didn't want any trouble. And so — don't say anything!

Someone has humorously predicted that the next Council would produce only one article, but that it would be definitive. After that there would be no more meetings and "Si quis aliquid dixerit, anathema sit" — "If anyone says *anything,* let him be anathema." That would guarantee everlasting tranquillity. The priests could then content themsevles with saying nothing, or with saying things that mean nothing. There would be peace in the Church and even in the parishes! Everybody would be in seventh heaven, dripping with piety! Everyone would love one another. . . .

To return to the mode of our prayer: pay attention to your conception of prayer. Perhaps what I am going to say on this subject will upset you a bit, but you are free not to accept it. All I ask is that you attend to what I have to say and let it end up where it belongs — and if you think it is rubbish, throw it in the trash can; but I hope that first you will think it over carefully.

Just as an enormous amount of paganism, atheism and natural religion have been re-introduced these days under the cover of the Christian religion, so the same thing has happened in prayer. There is pagan prayer and there is Christian prayer, and the two are completely different.

The Apostles prayed long and hard. I don't know how many prayers they had recited when Christ told them at the end of his life: "You have never prayed. You don't know how to pray. You have never prayed in the right way, but now I shall teach you a prayer: Everything that you ask in my name you shall receive. Until now you haven't asked for anything in the right way."

Christian prayer is totally different from pagan prayer. This is something that has not yet been sufficiently realized.

The Apostles must have been shocked when they first heard Christ say: "Until now you haven't asked for anything in the right way." It's incredible! All those hours spent in adoration gone for nothing! People shouldn't say such things! They ought to have a little more respect for the peace and contemplation of others! But Christ said to them: "You haven't asked for anything in the

17

right way. I shall teach you a new prayer."

Let us try to outline for ourselves what this true Christian prayer is. We should have long ago outgrown the idea that we must pray in order to change God. Still this idea keeps coming back — the idea that prayer will make a rather absent-minded God pay attention, that it will convey information to a God who is ignorant, move a God who is rather cold-hearted — if if God were a motor that needs to be warmed up before you can use it.

We know that that is the wrong way to pray, but nevertheless our prayers are too frequently expressed in those terms. Too often we begin by praying in the wrong way. Look at all those prayers — "Spread, O Lord, thy grace within our souls" and so on. But let's be serious! Don't you believe that God is already doing just that?

What we should do is express our prayers in positive terms. "O Lord, you are spreading your grace in our souls, we would like to realize it and open ourselves to it."

Are you going to change God?

Our prayers are often expressed to God in the imperative. It's disgraceful. But since we never think when we pray, or how we pray, it's a disgrace that's easy to go along with. And so we give God advice and tell Him what to do — "O Lord, have pity! Don't forget us! Don't lose your memory — and after all, at your age, there's some danger of that happening!"

But as soon as one begins to think, that sort of thing stops. As soon as one begins to think, there is no prayer that does not ask a question.

There is only one person who ought to be changed by prayer, and that is the person who is praying.

We behave like the rooster Chanticleer who thought that his crowing made the sun rise and that if he didn't crow there would be no sun. But it is the sun that makes Chanticleer rise. When you go to pray you should utter cries of joy. God has already worked one miracle in you by bringing you to church or by bringing you to prayer. And then if, instead of leaving off as soon as you can (which is evidently what you are tempted to do) you sit down and make yourself continue, perhaps He will have the time to tell you what He wants to say to you. And God is much more anxious to speak to you than you are to listen to Him.

You are not God, He is. You are not good,

He is. You may not want God, but God wants you.

As Pascal said: *It is not man who prays to God and is not heard; it is God who prays to man and is not heard.*

It is God who wants to give, it is you who do not want to receive.

To pray is to open yourself little by little to what you are asking.

It is only by grace that you pray. You believe in what is technically called prevenient grace; you believe that you can do nothing in the religious domain without grace; here is an application of that belief.

What is this new prayer that Christ taught his Apostles: "to pray in his name?" It's not a mere formula. It means to pray in the name of the Son. And what does "in the name" mean? It means in a filial state. And what does "in a filial state" mean? It means under the guidance of the Holy Spirit which leads our hearts to cry out "Father!"

And so to pray is to change gear. In ordinary circumstances it is you who thinks, you who acts, you who wishes. But from the moment that you begin to pray you must put yourself under the guidance of the Holy Spirit, you must listen to someone, you must change gear; and that takes time and means being submissive.

A Trappist friend of mine once said: "There's no point in parking your car if you leave your engine running at full speed." Your engine is your spirit. You go to church and park your car, but you leave your motor running at full speed; in other words you are still geared to your speed, your rhythm, your will, your desires. God can't change gear — it would grind the works. You must slow down, change speed, gear yourself to the Holy Spirit. You should adjust your speed to His speed, your rhythm to His rhythm, your will to His will.

What is truly divine in prayer is that, like all the sacraments, it leads through a death to a resurrection.

That is the essence of the Christian life — to die to oneself and to resurrect in God. To live in God. All the sacraments do that. The essence of the sacraments — baptism, confession, the eucharist — is participation in the death and resurrection of Christ. And prayer is perhaps the most overwhelming process of death and resurrection.

Everyone who prays begins by asking for something that he wants, something that he has set his heart on; but if he prays truly by the time he has finished he will have set his heart not on the thing that he was asking for but on Him of whom he was asking it.

One begins by wanting something from God and trying to run away from Him as soon as one has got it. But every prayer of entreaty ought to end as a prayer of trust, of putting the matter into the hands of God: "Thy will be done."

Every prayer begins "My will be done" and every true prayer ends "not my will by Thine be done."

Every prayer begins like Christ's. He himself began by asking for something that he should not have asked for. "Father, if thou art willing, remove this cup from me. Father, if thou art willing, remove this cup from me. Father, if thou art willing, remove this cup from me." And he said that for a whole night, a whole night, a whole night. For a whole night he asked for something that he should not have asked for. One always has to begin like that, but when one prays truly one moves on to a more profound prayer, and one finishes by getting up and saying "And yet not my will but Thine be done."

One begins by being attached to the thing one is asking for; but when true prayer has done its work, one has trust and confidence and faith in Him of whom one was asking it.

There are those who have eyes only for the gifts of this world, and to these people the gifts are never enough, never sufficient to insure their independence. But there are others who lift their eyes toward the face of the Giver and see such peace that they are happy forever, they need nothing else because He is there. Once you have said "Father" there is nothing else to say. If He is the Father what else could you want to say? Once you have said "Father" you can never go beyond that.

To die and be resurrected. When you pray you should die in a whole part of yourself where you are completely alive — in your fears, your desires, your anxieties, your demands, your irritations, your stupid resentment against everything — and you should be resurrected in a whole part of yourself where you are dead — in that part where there is peace, joy, patience, faith, forbearance, goodwill, kindness, forgiveness, serenity and trust to go on believing in the dark in what you have seen in the light. Death and resurrection. It is an experience that you should try.

For me, faith is always something to be experienced. You should never accept mechan-

23

ically what you are told about God. If I recite the Apostle's Creed I am refusing not to believe, I don't want not to believe. But to believe positively is to put some meaning into it, it is to experience that it is true. For my part I believe because of my experience. There are still a lot of things that I haven't experienced, but it is up to me to try them one day. And you should try them too.

The woman of Samaria said: "Come and see. Come and try. Come and see a man who has told me all that I have ever done. Perhaps he will help you to understand yourselves. Try. Try. He is frank and sincere with unbelievers, but try him yourselves, there is no need to believe me. Try him. Pray."

The basic idea of pagan prayer is that prayer will change God. But when you pray as a Christian it is you who are opening yourself to God's prayer. And that brings about a complete change in the style of your prayers. Every prayer becomes an act of faith, an act of trust.

That is the prayer for oneself. The prayer for oneself is very straightforward; it is God asking you to open yourself to Him, it is God praying to you. You will never ask God the hundredth part of what He wants to give you.

Then there is the prayer for others, and that is a very serious problem, for all too often the prayer for others is a canker in Christianity, an appalling alibi. "I will pray for you!" When you hear someone say that you know that he won't lift a finger to help you, that he feels free of any obligation to do anything. He will pray for you! It's frightening when someone says that to you because then you can be sure that your case is desperate and that the other person isn't going to do a single thing. The alibi of prayer ... !

We are responsible for God's honor.

God created an instrument of salvation to grant prayers, and that instrument is you. He created an instrument of salvation for granting forgiveness, and that instrument is you. Do you forgive your fellow-men ? *I will forgive you if you will forgive each other.* The pardon of our fellow-men is the sacrament of God's pardon.

It is up to you to deliver yourselves from evil. It is up to man to create whatever is needed to deliver the world from evil — education, medicine, technology, science, engineering. To work !

25

THE PRAYER OF A MODERN MAN

Prayer becomes nothing more than a shameful alibi when it is used for unloading onto God what one ought to be doing oneself. That is something that modern man detests. Modern man no longer prays God to do something that he ought to do himself.

There is nothing purely spiritual in the Church. Nothing in the world is purely spiritual. The order of the Church is not materialist, but it is not idealist either; it is sacramentalist. There is always a visible sign. The Church herself is a sacrament, a visible sign of the presence of God, of the word of God, of the love of God in the world. That is what the Church should be.

Every time that you pray for someone else, the proper effect of that prayer should be to make you do something for that person.

The Church is a visible sign given by God of His presence in the world. It is through the charity of the Church that people believe in the charity of God. It is through the bread of the Church that people will believe in the bread of God. Everything else is suspect, everything else reeks of alibi. There is always something that can be done. Always, even if it is only very little.

To be sure we must all pray for one another, but the real mark of sincerity is that our prayers should lead us to do something — write a letter, send a book, give a sign, make a phone call, do something, no matter what, so long as it is a visible sign. I believe that grace is conveyed by the sacraments. And if you believe that, it will make you clear away a whole area that has been lying fallow around you and which, because of a false conception of prayer, has unfortunately remained uncultivated.

To pray is to open ourselves to God so that He can open us to others.

Why do we blame the Pharisee? Because he refuses to receive from God, and so is unable to give to others; because he does not feel the mercy that God has for him, and so has no pity for sinners; because he does not open himself to God, and so does not open himself to others.

God does not want worshippers, thank you very much. He wants collaborators. Let me advise young men not to marry women who worship them, for nothing is more wearying. At first, of course, it's all very flattering, but after a while. . . . Instead marry someone who will work with you. To be sure you will have moments of intimacy and contemplation when you reflect on the joy you have in working together, but if you spend all your time reflecting on this joy there will be no more work! Think about that. There is nothing more harmful in Christianity than a certain idea of contemplation, a certain type of quietism.

There is one question that should be put to all contemplatives: what God are you contemplating? The answer is in the Gospel: "No one has at any time seen God." God is in the clouds! Nobody has ever seen Him.

"The only-begotten Son, who is in the bosom of the Father, he has revealed him." You can contemplate only one true God, the God incarnate. You can contemplate only Jesus Christ. Beyond that there is no salvation. There is only one name that has been given to men by which they might be saved. So whom do you contemplate? The God who is the Savior, the God who is the Redeemer, the God who gives His life, the God who gives Himself to the utmost of His strength, even to death? Whom do you contemplate? The God who serves you?

Then how is it possible for you to contemplate Him sincerely and not be led to do as He does?

How can you contemplate a God who is

unceasingly active by remaining in your contemplation?

What is the only order that Jesus gave to Mary Magdalene, the patron of contemplatives? "Go to your brothers." But first of all He received her, preached to her, because she was beside herself. She had to remain a long time in adoration to let her feelings become like Christ's, for the peace of Christ to become her peace, for the love of Christ to become her love, for the joy of Christ to become her joy, for the trust of Christ to become her trust and for the reverence of Christ to become her reverence.

After that everything is all right. You can go. Everything is in its proper place. Prayer has become active. Prayer is involved in life. Faith is committed.

Let me put this as clearly as I can. The more you travel the more you should consult the map. There's no doubt that you ought to travel, for that's one of the purposes of life, but so many people say to me: "I travel so much that I haven't got time to look at the map anymore. I haven't got time to pray." And my reply to these people is: "Then you will never arrive anywhere. The more you drive around the more often you should stop. Why? To find out where you've come from and where you're going."

The best definition I know of prayer, and the one that fits in best with what I have been saying to you about the word of God and about vocation, is this:

Prayer is a realization of the call of God in our lives.

Prayer is a realization of our Christian vocation.

That's all there is to it, but it takes a long time to realize that God is speaking and to realize the direction in which He is calling us. Above all it is a realization of the duty to act. That is the union between prayer and action. Contemplation is a terrible thing.

Christianity is neither contemplation nor action. It is participation. Contemplation is looking at God as if He were an object. But if you participate in God in the sense that you let yourself be penetrated by Him, you will go to the cross like Him, you will go to work like Him, you will clean shoes, do the washing up and the cooking, all like Him. You cannot do otherwise because you will have become part of Him. You will do what He loves to do.

People sometimes ask me how long they

should spend praying. How on earth should I reply to a question like that? It depends on how you travel. If you are on the highway — and there are times in life when you are on the highway, when you are constantly with God — then there is no need to pray. There's no need to stop and look at the the map when you're on a highway because your route is clearly marked. But there are times when you are on the back roads, and then you have to keep stopping all the time. There are times when you are completely lost and you have to spend half an hour studying your map trying to find out where you are. So it all depends on how things are going and each person should spend as long in prayer as he needs.

Action and contemplation are not two separate and distinct fuctions of the Christian life, they are two different aspects. Everybody should be both active and contemplative. Everybody should consult the map as he travels along. There are people who need to consult it for a long time and there are others for whom a quick glance is enough.

When I read the lives of the saints I've often noticed how at the beginning of their lives they spent a long time studying the map and how at the end they spent most of their time traveling. Read Charles de Foucauld. But don't begin by doing a lot of traveling, don't you begin at the point where the saints ended, because if you do you will find yourself going 'round in circles.

Most modern Christians are like musicians who are so eager to get on with the concert that they can never be bothered to wait and tune their instruments. They want to launch into action right away, so they play their instruments horribly out of tune. They think that they are giving everyone a great deal of pleasure but in fact they are boring everyone to death. They go out and buttonhole everyone in sight. They try to meet everyone. They rush off to save the whole world.

Instead, go and hide. Tune your instrument. Go and consult the map — and sometimes it will take a very long time to find your place on the map. There are so many people nowadays who have even lost the map.

But prayer in life, life in prayer; prayer in action, action in prayer — they are all one. It's a terrible mistake to divide them.

To pray is to consult your Christian vocation.

If you don't believe that God is in your life, then it's a waste of time to look for Him in your prayers. It's because I know that God is in my life, is calling me and speaking to me, that I know it's worth listening to Him. It's because He is in my life, because He has a plan for my life, a vocation for me, that it's worth listening to Him, for He knows better than I do what is good for me and where I ought to go. And so I listen to Him. But if He isn't in your life, then there is not the remotest chance that He will be in your prayers.

What does praying for others really mean?

I began by saying that it means letting yourself be filled with the love of God for them. A love which is active and ready to sacrifice its life. A love which is sacramental, or in other words, a love which should always be expressed by an outward, visible sign.

I believe that love, in itself, is communicative. The only thing that can be really communicated is love. I believe that love has an immediate effect on other people. From the moment that you really love someone, you are capable of doing anything for that person. I believe that it is this love that creates miracles. Love and faith are the causes of miracles — and they are the direct causes; it is not something which is routed through God, it is not God who works miracles. Since love is of God and you are of God, it is you who work miracles. When you love someone, your love can be felt; and the other person feels it immediately too. If the physicists and technologists want to claim that love is transmitted by waves I am quite happy to go along with them; it wouldn't surprise me in the least. What I mean is that when someone is looking at you behind your back, you will, if you are at all sensitive, feel it and turn around. There is more communication going on between us than you think; and if someone loves you, you can feel it with your eyes shut. And if someone doesn't love you you can feel that too with your eyes shut, just as I can tell how my listeners are reacting to what I say without my having to look at them because I can sense their waves. Love is something that you can feel with your eyes shut, it works directly. But though love communicates directly, it can do so only if it is sincere, only if it is active, because if it is alibi-love it is not true love. If you say, "I will pray for you," you are not showing a sincere interest in that person if you think that your prayer is enough in itself and that you are excused from actually doing anything; but if you mean "I am going to put myself in such a loving disposition toward you that I will do anything for you," then your love is active. You can see the difference. Your love is active only because it is sincere and because you really are prepared to do anything.

And now, though it might cause you some difficulties, let me conclude with an analogy: there's no difference between offering one's suffering and offering one's prayers. Both are useless.

Only love can be communicated.

Only love is active.

Suffering is not active, and I hope that it cannot be communicated.

Love, when it is sincere, is communicative, immediately communicative. It can work miracles. It can raise the dead. You ought to have no doubts on that score. You are responsible for everyone around you. If they are happy and in good health it's because you love them sufficiently. That should be the measure of your responsibility. A Christian is responsible for the salvation of the world. You will save all those whom you love sufficiently. You will take with you all those to whom you are sufficiently attached. If you die at this moment, whom will you take with you? If you depart this life alone, you are damned. Whom do you need in order to win eternity for yourself? That is a question a Christian should ask himself. If you say: "I pray for everyone but I need no one," then you are damned. That is using prayer as an alibi. That is reducing prayer to mumbo-jumbo.

For my own part I know that I need everyone. I want everyone to be saved. I don't want to be saved alone. Every day at mass I pray for the salvation of the whole world.

Only love is communicative. Don't make an offering of your suffering. That's the last thing to offer. Suffering is evil. If you believe that suffering is good, that it has some value, then you should increase it, nurture it. Unfortunately, there are Christians who do just that — they go on pilgrimages barefoot, they stick pins in their behinds, they put stones in their shoes, and they think that all that pleases God. But why do they stop there? Why don't they spend all day walking around on their heads? They're missing a magnificent opportunity for acquiring merit. What a waste! All they need to do is spend all day banging their heads against a wall and they would win unlimited merit. And God would love that because God is a little Moloch who loves the smell of blood and smoke and suffering!

You can only make an offering of suffering,

if suffering has some value. But if suffering were valuable, then Christ would have said, "Suffer, and make one another suffer." Unfortunately that is what we in fact too often do — but without Christ's commandment.

You should offer neither your suffering nor your prayers. You should love, and love will lead you to action. Look at Christ. That's all I need say. If He thought that He could save the world by contemplation alone He would have stayed with his Father where He could contemplate as much as He pleased in peace. But it is love that saves the world, and love is active. But in order to save the world with the love of God, with the heart of God, with the devotion of God, with the reverence of God, with the humility of God, go now and worship Him.

God Invites Us
To Be Men

One of the more serious charges leveled against Christians by the modern world, and especially by the psychologists and psychoanalysts, is the ambiguity of their recourse to the Father — "Our Father who art in Heaven." Can a man (they ask) be filial without being infantile?

Are we Christians authorized (or condemned) to remain forever children because we have a Father, and a Father who is all-powerful? His knowledge makes up for our ignorance and His strength for our weakness. We are allowed to remain small, ignorant, passive and submissive because we put our trust in Him "who knows best" and "without Whom we are capable of nothing" and Who can do in us, and in the world around us, what we renounce doing for ourselves. If man raises himself up, God will humble him, but if man humbles himself, God will raise him up.

Such a religion would appear to deprive man of his manhood. It would seem to be, as the Marxists maintain, an alienation of the creature in the hands of the Creator. Teilhard de Chardin defined the sickness of our times by saying that those who have faith in God do not seem to have faith in man and, in consequence, those who have faith in man distrust faith in God.

"The great complaint of the atheists is that the religious man does not carry human effort to its utmost limit from reverence or fear of God, or even from laziness, he is conservative; he waits for God to do what he ought to do for himself. Anything that he can't understand he puts down as 'providential.' He thinks that God will do whatever he is incapable of doing himself."

And so God becomes the compensation for our weaknesses; but in that case it follows that God retreats as man advances. Hence the contemporary atheism based on the rediscovery of the dignity and creative vocation of man.

For a real man the worst vice is resignation. But has not Christianity long been preached as the religion of resignation, of failure, of the Cross?

Let me attempt to outline a reply.

Yes, there is a way of being filial and also of being adult.

Remember that every man is faced with this problem, for every man is a son before he becomes a father. And it is not necessary that he should cease being a son in order to become a father; it is enough that he should be a real father. It is not necessary, as the psychoanalytic slogan about "the murder of the Father" has it, to deny or kill one's father in order to become a father oneself. So in fact this problem which is supposed to apply only to Christians applies to everybody.

Therefore I shall reply to both the human question and the religious one; and I shall divide my reply into two points:

1. One becomes adult in relation to one's Father when one no longer expects anything from Him.

Does that mean that we should expect nothing from God? Yes, indeed, for I believe that one of the conditions of being an adult is not to hanker for gifts, not to count on

41

someone else to carry out your own responsibilities, not to avoid your duty to think and do and try by putting yourself under the protection of God and relying on His generosity.

God is not man's alibi — an excuse for not being a man. God is man's Creator and Father. All the doctrines of "substitution" are degrading: "Christ suffered for us. Jesus died in our place. He expiated our sins." This way of understanding the Redemption disgusts modern man. Say rather: "Christ did not suffer in order that we should not suffer. Christ did not die in order that we should not die. He suffered and He died in order that our suffering and our death should be like His — full of love and hope and faith!"

A certain kind of prayer of entreaty degrades man. I once heard a theologian reply to the objection "prayer cannot change God nor alter His plans" by quoting St. Thomas: "God has decided from all eternity to grant His grace only in answer to prayer." This puts man in the position of being an eternal beggar. Be good, and you will be given candy.

How much more healthy and true it is to say to men: "Be careful, for what you ask of God, God has only you to do it!"

2. Because God has given us everything,

and we need nothing further, prayer to God makes us more manly.

A real father is one who has revealed himself so completely and communicated so well with his son that his son finds himself capable of becoming a father in his turn.

The real filial prayer (and therefore the real adult prayer), the real Christian prayer, is one of complete trust, of pride, of thanksgiving: "Father, I bless you . . . Father, I thank you . . . Father, I know that you always hear my prayers . . . Father, everything that is thine is mine. . . ." And when the Son, or the sons, say that and add: "and everything that is mine is thine," what they are expressing is their identification with the Father. For what belongs to God is the ability to love and to give. And so if they have received everything from God, they have also received the ability to do as He does. He has given them the gift of giving.

Every Christian prayer is a prayer of thanksgiving — and since we are told to offer such prayers "at all times and in all places," one wonders where and when one could make any other kind of prayer! The prayer of thanksgiving is to become aware of the gift of God. "If you knew the gift of God. . . ." We will never ask as much of God as He has given us. It is He who wants to give and we who refuse to receive. It is God who is praying to men and whose prayers are not heard. God is a real Father. We cannot even ask Him for something without finding that He has already offered it.

Nothing could be more pagan than the old tag: "Man proposes and God disposes." That makes God into an arbitrary and despotic master and man into a timorous and suppliant slave. The truth and pride of Christianity is this: "God proposes and man disposes." God is our Father, God is giving, but He respects the liberty of man. He does not even force His gifts on man. And when man "asks" for something, he is in fact only opening himself to the entreaty of God. Man is then granting God's prayer.

Understood in this sense, prayer makes man more manly; it makes us aware of our filial dignity and reveals to us our strength and responsibilities.

Every Christian prayer is an inventory, an enumeration, a stock-taking of all that God has done for us. Every prayer is a *Magnificat, Benedictus, Credo, Gloria in excelsis, Sanctus, Te Deum, Gloria Patri, et Filio, et Spiritui Sancto*. Every prayer is Eucharistic, that is to say, a recognition — recognition in the dual meaning of knowledge and gratitude.

And every prayer is related to action, for prayer is acceptance of God's plan; and God wants us to be fathers in our turn and do for others what He has done for us.

No, I expect nothing from God. No, I am not relying on God to do the things that I ought to do for myself. God is of no use to me. God is useless. For God has achieved the highest aim of the intelligent educator, which is to bring His pupil to the point where he can do without Him.

But everything that I have, I have from God. Everything that is best in me comes from Him. All that is most living in me I have received from Him, and when I consult the depths of my being the voice that I hear would not be so truly my own if it did not speak to me so much of Him. Nothing is more necessary to me than to keep counting my riches and convincing myself of my freedom and responsibilities by measuring the extent of God's withdrawal from me.

At that moment our relations with God become free. God no longer prevents us from becoming men; rather He invites us to do so.

The joy of the Father is to have communicated so well with His son that His son becomes a better Father to other men than He. The Creator tells us: "Rule the earth and make it subservient to you," or in other words: "Finish the work I began, do it better than I!" And the Redeemer said: "You will do greater things than I."

Remember our earthly fathers. So long as we were dependent on them, we felt irritable and rebellious, for one can love properly only when free. But once they gave us our freedom our relations with our parents became much happier; we turned back to them with gratitude and joy, we asked for their advice as equals and benefited from doing so. And when we found them again, we became aware of all that they had given us, and we realized that we would not be so alive if their lives had not, in a very real sense, become our own.

God Leaves Us Free

God is not a judge. God judges no one. God will never punish you nor damn you nor condemn you.

Is such a picture of God atheistic? (For man becomes an atheist from the moment he begins to think of himself as being better than the God he serves, and what man would be willing to condemn thousands of his fellow-men to everlasting suffering for having committed passing sins?)

Christ said: "I judge no one" and "Neither does the Father judge any man." "For God did not send His Son into the world in order to judge the world."

Then how will we be judged? "And if anyone hears my words, and does not keep them, it is not I who judge him; for I have not come to judge the world, but to save the world. He who rejects me, and does not accept my words, has one to condemn him. The word that I have spoken will condemn him on the last day." So everyone is his own judge, punishing or condemning himself by his response to the Word of God.

Moreover, John said that the Judgment had already taken place: "The light has come into the world, yet men have loved the darkness rather than the light, for their works were evil."

We must be careful to rid ourselves of the popular picture of God as a Judge. There are those who think that the aim of religious education is to wedge man in between God the all-powerful Creator and God the inexorable Judge; but the only result of this is to prevent man from ever loving God.

All the Christian education of my youth tended toward making me believe that God could not be harmed, but that He could do us harm.

And everything that the Gospel has taught me is that God will never harm us, but that we can harm Him.

Choose the God you believe in and reject the one you don't.

Christ told us: "Love your enemies. Do

good to those who hate you. Pray for those who persecute you."

Nobody believes it, but God has really done what He orders us to do.

In my youth whenever I suffered a humiliation or a failure, because I was brought up religiously, I immediately asked myself: "What can I have done to God to make Him punish me like that?" And I always found something.

But since reading the Gospel, whenever I hear a piece of good news or unexpectedly meet a friend or receive some praise, I say to myself: "What sin have I committed to make God be so nice to me? He loves His enemies, He does good to them that hurt Him. . . ."

And don't run away with the idea that when Christ gave us that commandment he was creating artificial difficulties in order to make the road to salvation more meritorious. Far from it. When he revealed the Beatitudes, Christ was telling us about God, about the way God feels, about His character, habits, tastes. "You will be like the Father. . . ."

Those who make God a Judge are also making Him a pagan and a sinner. For Christ said: "If you love those who love you, what merit have you? For even sinners love those who love them. And if you do good to those who do good to you, what merit have you? For even sinners do that. And if you lend to those from whom you hope to receive in return, what merit have you? For even sinners lend to sinners that they may get back as much in return."

If God were a Judge who merely gave everyone his due and limited himself to a sort of debit and credit bookkeeping, then why not replace Him with an electronic computer? It's as if He were to say: "I'm willing to pay out what's due but after that we're quits, and I don't want anyone coming to me and asking for My sympathy for something extra."

But God is not just; He makes just. He does not confine Himself to keeping an account of merits and demerits, He does not limit Himself to punishing sinners. Instead He devotes Himself completely to making the sinner a saint, the unjust man a just man, the evil man a good man. Isn't that the only occupation worthy of God?

Be careful, for you will come to resemble the God of your imagination. And if you think that God is just, and nothing but just, then you will also think that you are doing a

religious deed when you bring your own little pebble to the stoning of the guilty — "I
am like God, I am just."

But Christ tells us: "Don't let yourself get
caught up in those vicious circles, in those
wretched situations where you say to someone, 'You did that to me so I'm going to do
this to you. You didn't help me so I'm not
going to help you.' For if you do that, then
you are imitating each other, not God; you
are behaving like tightfisted shopkeepers.
But instead lend your fountain pen to the
person who borrowed your ball-point and
didn't give it back; invite the person who
didn't invite you; astonish your enemy; create new, unpredictable, fertile situations.
Then you will be like the Father Who makes
His sun rise on the good and the evil, and
sends His rain on the just and the unjust."

No, God will not punish you, nor will He
reward you; but He will make you eternal.
Stop thinking of the last judgment as a sort
of enormous prize-giving where everyone
gets what he wants and goes where he
wants. For where your treasure is, there also
will be your heart and your soul and your
body.

All my early religious education led me to

believe that the damned would like to get out of hell but that God kept pushing them back down again, leaving them in their prison to be tortured.

But the Gospel (and even St. Thomas) have made me understand that God loves the damned. *It is the damned who do not love God.* If God were to impose Himself on them forcibly, they would suffer even more. So God, out of compassion, doesn't force them.

But, you will object, the Gospel is full of judgments, condemnations and punishments. True, but in each instance you should ask yourself this vital question: is God's judgment executive or declarative?

Let me explain. When Christ said: "Hand him over to the executioners . . . Throw him out . . . Bring my enemies here and cut their throats in front of me . . . ," do you think that his judgment was declarative, that is, revealing and making manifest the true state of that person; or was it executive, that is, intended to change that person's condition by taking away from him what he clung to and punishing him for his former pleasures?

For myself, I have no doubt that it not in the nature of my loving God to make sinners suffer more and be more unhappy than they already are. The divine light does not make the sinner wretched; all it does is show how wretched the sinner is.

Remember the parable of the unmerciful servant. Moved by compassion a king forgave a servant a debt of ten thousand talents. As he went out, the servant met a fellow-servant who owed him a hundred pennies, and at once he began to throttle him and had him thrown into prison until he had paid all his debt. And when the king heard of this, he handed the first servant over to the torturers until he had paid all *his* debt. Do you think that judgment was declarative or executive?

God loves, God forgives. There is only one thing He cannot forgive us, and that is not loving and not forgiving in our turn. He cannot force someone who doesn't love, who refuses to love, to be as if he did love. He cannot prevent us from becoming what we are destined to be. He cannot sanction our remaining in that terrible state of non-love.

And so when God realizes that in spite of all His forgiveness you have not learned to forgive, and that in spite of all His love you have not learned to love, don't think that He then withdraws His forgiveness or His love from you; but He is forced to recognize that

53

His forgiveness has had no effect on you, and that His love has not won you over, and that you have remained out of reach, unresponsive to what He has so often tried to communicate to you.

For there is only one sign that you have been forgiven, and that is that you should be able to forgive others in your turn. You have not really received forgiveness if you are not capable of giving it. You have not known God if you cannot love.

In the Gospel, Christ in his mercy is warning us of the consequences — disastrous or beatifying — of our choices. It is not He who makes them disastrous, but it is He who warns us that they can be disastrous, that it is a terrible thing to pass all eternity in a state where one hopes for nothing, is interested in nothing, loves nothing and no one. He does not make it terrible. He warns us that it will be terrible.

And yet countless numbers of Christians either gloat or give themselves a pleasurable fright at the prospect of God's punishment of sinners. Pascal went so far as to write: "For we do not see that God hates and scorns all sinners together so that even at the hour of their death, which is the time when their state is most miserable and wretched,

54

divine wisdom adds mockery and derision to the vengeance and fury which will condemn them to everlasting torture. . . ." And people are surprised that there are atheists!

Recently I was invited to Barcelona by the Jesuit student chaplains. At the end of my lecture, an old theologian got up to contradict me. "Father," he said, "do you deny what Benedict XV affirms in such-and-such a decree, that God positively punishes sinners? They are not only wretched because of their state, they will also expressly suffer divine punishment. I would lay down my life for that article of faith!"

"Father," I replied, "as any student of theology could easily tell you, divine laws are not like human laws, where the policeman chases the thief to prevent him from enjoying in peace the fruits of his crimes. The laws of God are the laws of our happiness. Things are not good or evil because God commands or forbids them. God commands them or forbids them because they are beneficial or harmful. If you go out of the sun and into the shade you will feel cool, and if you throw yourself into the water you will get wet. Why do so many Christians take pleasure in thinking that every now and then God visits those unhappy people who are drowning themselves and pushes them down a little further for the satisfaction of saying 'I told you so'?

"My God is love, and nothing but love. But love leaves you free, free to love and free not to love, and it would deny itself if it were to appeal to any authority other than that."

The Least of My People

During the Council forty bishops drawn from all the nations of the world met together once a week to study in depth an important question: to what extent is the Church now, and to what extent can and ought the Church to become in the future, the Church of the poor, the infirm, the crippled, the sick?

The Gospel is always new. The Beatitudes are there to be rediscovered. "Blessed are you poor, for yours in the kingdom of God." The Church is disturbed, the Church feels ill at ease when confronted with these words today, just as were many of those who heard them for the first time two thousand years ago.

Jesus identified himself with the Church: "He who listens to you, listens to me. He who scorns you, scorns me." But He also identified himself with the poor: "What you do to the least of my people, you do to me . . . He who gives even a glass of water to one of these little ones will not go without his reward."

Christ thus identified himself with the Church *and* with the poor.

Then how is it possible for the Church to be affluent and the poor without religion? One third of humanity enjoys two thirds of the world's resources, and that third is, for the most part, made up of Christians. The poor are the others. The Christians have the Gospel and prosperity; two thirds of the world have neither the one nor the other. The kingdom of God no longer belongs to the poor!

But the Church ought to be the Church of the poor. Her mission was to announce the Good News to the poor. The true manifestation of Christ, His messianic sign, was to evangelize the poor.

Remember the conversation with the disciples of John the Baptist. They asked Jesus: "Art thou He who is to come, or shall we look for another?" That is the question for all time: "Are you the real Church — the Church of liberation of the oppressed, the

58

Church of the poor? Or should we look else-
where? Shall we wait for another?"

And Jesus replied: "Go and report to John
what you have heard and seen: the blind
see, the lame walk, the lepers are cleansed,
the deaf hear, the dead rise, the poor have
the gospel preached to them." This last is
the sure sign, the sign that designates the
true Messiah and the true Church. Small
wonder that so many people find it difficult
to recognize them today.

Note how Christ's enumeration was in an
ascending order. To evangelize the poor was
even more miraculous than to raise the
dead. For the poor person is someone who
doesn't count in the eyes of men. When a
rich man dies, it is not hard to gather a few
people around his coffin and carry out some
ceremonies. But a poor person dies unnoticed. "If you want to become invisible,"
says a Spanish proverb, "become poor." Nobody will see you, nobody will notice you.

Which is why when God came into the
word He made Himself poor. He wanted a
poor family, a poor exterior, a poor condition in order to leave us free, terribly free,
to choose Him or ignore Him.

We still have that freedom today.

A person who is poor or sick is invisible

to the eyes of the rich and the healthy; he is someone who dies unnoticed, someone you have to seek out at his home.

The parable of Lazarus and the rich man shows us how easily we become blind to the poor. Why do we blame the rich man? He didn't steal from Lazarus, he didn't ruin him, he didn't even exploit him by employing him at a miserable salary for jobs that no one else would do. Quite simply, he didn't see Lazarus. The poor man is invisible ! It's like those people who say: "There are no poor people or serious invalids in my parish. . . ." And so because he didn't see Lazarus in his life-time, he will not see him for all eternity. The distance that he established between himself and the poor man has since become unbridgeable. For the distance that he established was between himself and God, because the Kingdom of God belongs to the poor and whoever cuts himself off from the poor cuts himself off from God.

And in the same way, why do we praise the Good Samaritan? Because he saw the poor man. The priest and the Levite had pretended not to see him and had passed by on the other side. But the Good Samaritan knew how to see the poor man; beyond the stranger, the political enemy and the heretic, beyond the "communist," the schismatic, and the "traitor" he saw a man who was suffering and needed him.

Where everyone else would have seen only an enemy he was able to see a "brother." He saw the man. And the Church should see all men, not as pagans or infidels or heretics or persecutors but as poor people who need her, even though they may distrust her.

For us also today, the sign that will conclusively reveal the divine nature of our apostolate is that we should go to the poor and the sick. Read Chapter 21 of St. Matthew, verses 14-16. Jesus entered Jerusalem on Palm Sunday and went into the Temple like the Master, like the Messiah. And what did He do? He drove out all those who were buying and selling, and then: "the blind and the lame came to him in the temple, and he healed them. But the chief priests and the Scribes, seeing the wonderful deeds that he did, and the children crying out in the temple, any saying 'Hosanna to the Son of David,' were indignant. . . ."

That is the messianic sign; he drove out the buyers and sellers, the rich, the money changers, all of them busy to the point of obsession with their speculations, and he went to the poor, busying himself with them and healing them. It was then that the children cried out: "Hosanna to the Son of David!"

We Christians also, if we busy ourselves with the poor, will shock people. "We shall be called the sons of God."

St. Luke is relentless when he describes the sort of invitations that we should give: "When thou givest a dinner or a supper, do not invite thy friends, or thy brethren, or thy relatives, or thy rich neighbors, lest perhaps they also invite thee in return, and a recompense be made to thee. But when thou givest a feast, invite the poor, the crippled, the lame, the blind; and blessed shalt thou be, because they have nothing to repay thee with; for thou shalt be repaid at the resurrection of the just."

The word of God is a terrible thing. Its mission is to make us poor by revealing to us how rich we in fact are. "I am the true vine, and my Father is the vine-dresser. Every branch in me that bears no fruit he will take away; and every branch that bears fruit he will cleanse, that it may bear more fruit. You are already clean because of the word that I have spoken to you." For the word of God raises doubts about ourselves; it makes us question and doubt ourselves, our virtues, our values, our worth; it prevents us from being satisfied with ourselves.

It is then that one understands the remark that Christ added to his message to John the Baptist: "And blessed is he who is not scandalized in me." Yes, indeed, blessed is he who is not repelled by the poor! Blessed is he who seeks out and loves and welcomes the poor man! Blessed is he who rejoices in the elevation of the poor—theirs is the Kingdom of God! Is that our beatitude?

But, it has been said, one can do something even finer for the poor than give them charity and make them share our wealth, and that is to make them aware of their own wealth. Once, when persecutors ordered him to hand over the treasures of the Church, St. Lawrence brought them the poor, the crippled and the infirm, saying: "Here are the riches of the Church!"

And now I would like to go into the meaning of this word of God more deeply.

Why this preference in the Gospel for the poor, the sinners and children over the rich, the just and adults?

Do the poor have a special value for us?

Is there, in the Church, some privilege attaching to economic poverty and physical suffering?

Yes, for isn't spiritual poverty much worse than economic poverty? And isn't spiritual suffering much more painful than physical suffering? The emotional poverty of a heart which cannot love nor make itself loved, poverty of intelligence, poverty of faith, indifference to the beauty of the world or to human tenderness — isn't all that infinitely more distressing than lack of money?

Moreover, as everyone knows, the poverty recommended by the Gospel is an attitude, a virtue. "Blessed are the poor in spirit."

Material poverty is a circumstance, and not a virtue. What is praised by the Lord is a condition of the heart, and not of the wallet. To be sure, true poverty, like good medicine, is psychosomatic. It is neither purely material, as in the case of those who say: "I no longer possess anything, I have given so much to the poor" (or "I have neglected to earn my living"). "I have sold my car; I have distributed my property; I have acquired poverty!"

Unfortunately, a poverty that has been acquired is a contradiction in terms; it can never be absolute. We could spend all our life trying to become poor, trying to rid ourselves of the very ambition to become poor and of our satisfaction at being poor. We can never be truly poor unless we are un- aware of it, unless we are so attached to the poor that they can strip us of all our posses- sions without our noticing it. Humility and poverty are among those curious virtues of which it has been said: "As soon as you think you have it, you don't have it."

Some of my colleagues do everything they can to imitate the Curé d'Ars. They go to great lengths to make themselves poor, but in the process of doing so they generally be- come impossible people. "Antisthenes," said a clear-sighted friend to the Cynic who was parading his poverty, "Antisthenes, I can see your pride through the holes in your cloak!"

Nor is true poverty purely spiritual.

Some people, after reading the above par- agraph, are likely to breath a sigh of relief. "How wonderful!" they'll say. "At last here's a preacher with some understanding! What a relief! He says it's enough to have the soul of a poor man, and that's just the case with me. I've dedicated all my property to the Lord — in spirit."

Very nice, but unfortunately the Pharisees had already thought of that one in the time of Christ as an excuse for not supporting their needy parents.

And so from time to time it would be a good idea to take a note out of your wallet just to make sure that, as the surgeons say, you are not suffering from adhesions. . . .

So much for the *virtue of poverty* — something which, it must be admitted, is as rare among the poor as among the rich. Nowadays anyone who wants to meet the poor in spirit must create his own public. Nobody is poor any longer; nobody accepts being poor or aims to be poor. Instead everyone is doing his utmost to deny his poverty and unhappiness and is wearing a mask of affluence, independence and contentment.

That is the reason why the apostle should approach people with the face of a poor man so that when confronted by him they will have the courage to take off their masks and to believe that it is possible to accept poverty, to look it in the face, since the apostle has found the means of bearing his poverty with serenity.

But if this virtue of poverty is rare, if it can be found among the rich as well as among the poor, let us return to our problem and ask ourselves what is the privilege of the state of *poverty*, and in particular of the state of material poverty; and let us also ask ourselves what is the privilege of the state of physical suffering.

It's not easy to define. For in the last analysis, God wants us to deliver others from these misfortunes and also protect ourselves from them. Surely the aim of Christian charity is that the rich should gain the soul of the poor but without losing all their property and that the poor should enjoy prosperity but without losing their souls, and that the sick should be cured.

And so, once again, what is there so wonderful about being in a poor state of health or in poor economic circumstances?

Let's begin by getting rid of the false answers. To begin with there's the old one that says: "Suffering is good."

No, suffering is not good. It is something to be fought against and overcome. Suffering diminishes man; it obsesses him, embitters him, revolts him.

No doubt it can be the occasion for spiritual insights or provide the sufferer with the opportunity to overcome his suffering, for rising above himself. Suffering sometimes leads people to call on profound resources

which healthy people generally leave un-
developed.

But suffering does not automatically have
this effect, or at any rate no more so than
does spiritual suffering.

But isn't suffering good because God sends
it either as a punishment or as a test?

No, God does not send suffering. Sickness
and death came into the world as a result of
man's sin, and they are allotted without any
system or regard to merit. They strike indif-
ferently at the good and the evil, though
with a slight preference for the good since,
as the English say, if God sends His rain
down on the just as well as on the unjust,
it's the just man who gets wetter because the
unjust man has stolen his umbrella. . . .

To make God the immediate cause of
everything that happens is "providentialism."
God permits suffering, but He does not want
it and even less does He cause it.

So let us not say: "He who loves well punishes well. You are suffering because you are
favored of God."

Read the Gospel. Christ loved greatly, but
he punished no one. He cured the sick; he
wept over the sins of Jerusalem; he inter-
ceded for the forgiveness of his executioners.

Don't say: "God has taken your little child

. . . God has come to fetch your husband."

God neither created nor wished for death. He deplores it and, far from sending it to us, has done everything possible to overcome it.

Read the Gospel. Christ wept over the death of Lazarus, just as he weeps over the death of every one of us. He identified himself with our suffering and our death in order to free us of them. He gave the son back to his mother (the widow of Naim), the daughter back to her father (Jairus) and the brother to his sisters.

No, it is not Christ who takes your little child from you; but it is Christ who will give him back to you; for Christ so suffered and fought against the evil in man that He has the power to reunite you with him forever.

The vocabulary and popular conceptions used about God need to be revised. "God who punishes . . . Little Jesus will punish you . . . God wanted this, God did not permit that . . . God makes those he loves suffer."

No, God makes those he loves love, and *that* often makes them suffer. . . .

It's very dangerous to have mistaken ideas about God, for you will end up by resembling them. If you think that God punishes and chastises people and makes people suffer, then you run the risk of behaving in the same way. You will think that you are performing a religious deed when you add your own little pebble to the stoning of the "guilty" or when — out of love! — you increase the number of suffering people.

Who among us bases his life on the joy of believing in a God who is infinitely better than we are, infinitely more tender, more merciful, more gentle? That is the Good News that we ought to announce to the world, and not this judge and executioner.

No, there is no divine origin to suffering.

But there is a divine usage to which all suffering, like all sin and failure, can be put.

Because of our sins great misfortune has entered the world, but God offers us a grace of faith and love which is even greater. God does not send suffering, but He does invite us to make good use of it. Whenever a physical or moral catastrophe befalls us, God — who has so wonderfully created the dignity of human nature but who has also even more wonderfully restored it — offers us a destiny which is even finer, happier, more profoundly believing and loving than if we had not sinned or suffered.

Felix culpa!

Let us not go to those who are sick and

console them cheaply by telling them that it is God who has made them sick . . . and for their own good!

God loves them and helps them even more because they are sick, but they did not fall sick because God loves them.

God identifies himself closely with those who are weeping and suffering. But He does not make them weep or suffer.

God struggles with them against their sickness and against the sickness of the world, and He is working to free them from it.

But let us answer our problem: what is the privilege of the sick and the poor, of the state of physical suffering and economic poverty?

The answer is that they constitute a disposition to receive, they put people into a state of receptivity. They are valuable because they are means of revealing the truth.

Spiritual suffering and spiritual poverty are things that can always be denied. People can turn their attention away from them and pretend to ignore them. And that is what we all do. We pretend to be happy, upright, honest, content and independent, needing nothing and nobody.

But physical suffering and economic poverty are things which cannot be denied, cannot be hidden. People suffering from them are compelled to admit that they need help.

And so the poor and the sick are sacraments, the outward and visible signs, the revelations of our real condition. All humanity is poor and all humanity is sick. With respect and love it ought to recognize itself in those who present to it their true face.

Every man is poor, every man is sick, every man needs to be redeemed, healed, forgiven, granted grace.

We Christians say that faith, hope and charity are theological virtues, that is to say that we would be incapable of an act of true love, faith or hope were it not for the grace of God. Even with those we love the most — our husbands, our wives, our families, our children — even with them we are so poor in love, so quickly upset by impatience, anger, exhaustion or resentment that if God does not come into our hearts we cannot love them fully.

The poor, in the Church, are the witnesses, the revelation of our condition to everyone. The sick have no monopoly of sickness, nor do the poor have a monopoly of poverty. They are men like everyone else. But with this single difference — that they know their true condition whereas everyone else pretends not to know it.

The poorest person, the sickest person is not the one you think. The person who is most deaf is the one who does not know that he is deaf, the one who has not been delivered by baptism from the hardness of his heart toward God. The person who is most blind is the one who thinks he can see, whereas he cannot.

The sick are not people in a special category, cripples who are excluded from human society, "privileged" exceptions. And we who come to tend them are not rich or healthy or "normal."

They are our *brothers*; they show us the truth of man, the true face of humanity that has been wounded but can be cured. And if we have a service to render them, then they too have a service to render us, a truth to teach us. Our relations with them are based not on "charity" but on sharing.

Let us avoid saying stupid things like: "You're lucky, you have been chosen by God. You are piling up merits because of your suffering."

Rather let us say to them: "You are what I am and there is much that you can teach me.

I have come to you to deepen my own experience by listening to yours."

Because they are accustomed to suffering — "the familiars of pain" as Isaiah calls them — their attitude toward it is more just and sincere than is ours. We are always trying to escape it and turn our attention away from it; but they are plunged deep in it and have had to think about it, and so they have come closer to the truth, they have learned to appeal not only to the cares and attentions of their brothers but also to the mercy and grace of another Brother.

Blessed, I say, is he who knows that he has need of Another in order to be blessed!

Blessed is he who is incapable of being blessed by himself and for himself alone!

Blessed is he who is not of this world, who knows that "there is something rotten in the Kingdom of this world," who knows that there must be another world and another kingdom.

Blessed is he who hungers and thirsts for justice and who appeals to a higher, truer justice.

They are the ones whose *material state* leads them to welcome the gift of God. They have the chance to become poor but blessed, sick but blessed, suffering but blessed, if they are willing to turn to Him who offers them His love and His healing.

Then they will become Christians and apostles. We cannot be apostles if we are rich and happy or poor and unhappy; we can be apostles only when we have met Someone who is so alive and so good that He enables us to be poor and happy, Someone who is so great that in front of Him we discover how small we are — small but blessed — Someone so tender and merciful that He has made even our faults into happy faults.

The Christian religion is the religion of the poor, the small, of children and of sinners — of all those who have discovered that God is very great.

One day perhaps they will cease being poor, cease being sick, cease being children or sinners; but they will never cease being blessed because of Him in Whom they live forever.

The Scandal of
The Cross

No activity can be useful if it is not inspired by faith. No activity can be fruitful if it is not conceived in a sort of retreat of the personal will and in an attitude of attention and welcome to the will of God. Without this perpetual retreat from self and advance toward God, your ego will gradually spread and take over everything, and though you may think that you are filled with God, you will in fact be filled with yourself. Listen to God, consult God. "The Son can do nothing of himself." Christ revealed that he was in a state of constant attention to Another. We, too, should pay the same attention. You must be constantly expecting God. God does not conquer; He gives Himself. Be empty and expectant before Him. It is not up to you to produce the light; all you are expected to do is raise the shade. You cannot win God over or trap Him by a clever prayer. "God is not in the noise, the bustle or the will of man." At a given moment He will be there, but no one can say when that moment will come. For God is free.

There are some very intelligent people who cannot find God because they approach the truth with their intelligence only, intending to conquer it. But God gives Himself. It is very hard to become as a child if you are an intellectual. You must not even look for God, for you will never find Him; rather you must believe in Him. You must let Him reveal Himself to us. If you are used to thinking in terms of acquisition and merit, it is very hard to accept life and in the end to die. All too often people expect God to come like a judge riding on the clouds in the sky, majestic, regal, conquering. But God is already here on earth, and has always been here, hidden in the Bread, drunk in the Wine, scorned in the most insignificant of the people around us, attached to us so closely that when we look around to find Him we always overlook Him because He is so near.

But at a certain moment you will become

receptive to this eternal truth: you thought that you were looking for Him, but it was He Who was looking for you. You were trying to escape from your own life in order to find Him, but He had already entered your life. You were looking for Him in the future, and He is in the present. You wanted to go to heaven, but God has made Himself incarnate on earth.

The experience of St. Peter was like that: God was present even in the sinner. Peter protested: "Depart from me, for I am a sinful man, O Lord." He was saying: "My unworthiness excludes You and Your presence overwhelms me." He was rejecting that scandalous intimacy, that permanent presence of God in the sin and mediocrity of our lives.

For God is in our lives. Do not try to escape Him; instead, accept Him.

You cannot love and respect God more than you love and respect your own life, for you cannot have more respect for Him than you have for His will, for the mission that He has entrusted to you.

We should recognize God by the demands he makes on us. When Peter was called upon to play the part in the Church for which God had destined him, he had to begin by undergoing the experience of realizing that he was nothing. The Lord reduced him to nothing. We try to climb upon a pedestal, but the Lord likes to choose his apostles from the gutter. We say: "When I am a bit better . . . after the retreat . . . in two years' time . . . first I'm going to improve myself, then I'll present myself before Him . . . and it's beginning already . . . I feel that I am getting better. . . ." But by reaching down into the gutter, God makes sure that the person he chooses will not claim any merits for himself!

I am not saying that you should go and commit the same sins as before; but I am saying that you will always be sinners. We drink in sin like water. When you begin to discover that you are sinners, you should not think that you have become more wicked. All that has happened is that you have become more clear-sighted, and that is even a sign that you have become better. St. Teresa of Avila said: "Since becoming a Superior I commit many more sins, but I love the Lord much better." You will commit far fewer sins if you sterilize yourself, but you will also be moribund. It is not the elimination of sins that matters, but the growth of love.

"Perhaps you imagine," wrote C. S. Lewis

in *The Problem of Suffering*, "that this humility of the saints is a pious illusion which makes God smile. That would be an extremely dangerous mistake. It is dangerous in theory because it leads you to identify a virtue (i.e., a perfection) with an illusion (i.e., an imperfection), which is of necessity absurd. And it is dangerous in practice because it encourages a man to mistake the first glimmerings of light concerning his own corruption for the beginnings of a halo around his foolish head. No, you can be sure that when the saints say that they, even they, are full of sin, that they are recording the truth with a precision that is wholly scientific."

And when St. Paul discovered God, he also discovered that he was a sinner. The closer one is to God, the more one feels a sinner.

Think of how long it took the Apostles to discover God. How long do you think it will take you?

Let's be sincere — but, unfortunately, no one is sincere. Everyone decks himself out with affected emotions. Everyone pretends to believe. And the result is that no one believes. For too many Christians of good will Christianity consists of making believe — sometimes pretending to be sad, at other times pretending to be happy — but always with the gnawing certainty that none of that changes anything. How much I prefer to all that the sincere coarseness, the undisguised hardness of heart of the Apostles! How much more at ease do I find myself with these peasants who openly admit that they haven't understood a thing. What a relief they are after all the pious comedies and airs of earnest devotion. And how natural — and in a sense how reassuring too — our slowness to believe becomes set against the Apostles' candid admissions of their stupefying obtuseness, their determined resistance to the spiritual, their waterproof imperviousness to the divine.

They had the best teacher of religion in the world. Compare him with your own! They spent three uninterrupted years living with him, they were witnesses to all his miracles, to all his teachings, to his way of living. But — and don't forget this — they never understood a thing! They asked him questions after the most obvious parables, they put a low interpretation on the most spiritual doctrines and they tried to use him for their own ends while thinking that they were honoring him. Just think how shocked they were by the Passion. Jesus had foretold it to them; he had warned them in advance; he had even gone so far as to prophesy their reactions so that they might be able to find in their cowardice a reason for having faith in him. But none of it worked.

How hard they found it to believe in the Resurrection. How slow they were to accept it, how obstinate in their despair, how blind to the signs of the Resurrection. And how upset they were at the thought of the Ascension. Their last words to Christ after he had been resurrected and was on the point of ascending into heaven were a childish complaint: "Lord, wilt thou at this time restore the kingdom to Israel?" And they were left open-mouthed as all their hopes flew away with their Master: "Men of Galilee, why do you stand looking up to heaven?"

It does one good to think that they at least did not pretend to understand, to believe or to rejoice. They were sincere, they showed themselves for what they were, and that is why religion was able to take a hold on them and mark them forever. Compared with them who were so ponderous and slow, modern Christians seem to be charming but evasive and superficial. Each step forward that the Apostles took was a true one, a real one, and their faith was as sincere as their disbelief had been.

THE PRAYER OF A MODERN MAN

There was a wonderful man, John the Baptist. He is in a way the forerunner of every Christian, as he was of Christ. There is a permanent mystery of the forerunner in our souls, just as there is a permanent mystery of the motherhood of Mary. The Gospel reveals the perpetual immediacy of John the Baptist's mission: "There was a man, one sent from God, whose name was John. This man came as a witness, to bear witness concerning the light, that all might believe through him. He was not himself the light, but was to bear witness to the light."

The first annunciation of Christian salvation is the story of Zachariah. All his life Zachariah had been asking for a son, and when the Lord sent an angel to tell him that his wish had been granted, Zachariah exclaimed: "Impossible!"

But the trouble with Zachariah was that his prayer had not been granted at what he thought was the right time or in the right way. He had gone on praying, but he no longer believed in his prayer. A corpse lay between him and God. Between God and Zachariah, prayer had become an empty ceremony, a meaningless convention, like those reunions among families that are deeply divided: the relations still see each other, still smile at each other, even embrace each other when they meet, but there are many subjects that they no longer talk about because they know that they will never agree. The same thing happens in our relations with God; after disappointments and failures we still go on praying, we still go to mass and communion, but it's all dead, we don't expect anything to come from it, we no longer believe in it.

Zachariah is a strange type, but not at all unusual; he prayed, but at the same time he refused to believe in his prayers. He prayed for conscience's sake, but his heart was not in his prayers. He had to be punished in order to accept the gift of God and when he received what he had been asking for he was the first to be astonished. One sometimes prays in order not to stop praying, not to be not praying.

Look at the degree of hope that God expects of us. Even though you are eighty years old you should find nothing extraordinary in having a child. You are not open enough, not receptive enough, if you do not accept this, for everything is possible with God.

And there is something which is even more important for us, and that is one of the first sayings of John the Baptist: "In the midst of you there has stood one whom you do not know" (John 1:26). John the Baptist is a prophet, and that means that what he experienced concerns you. His words are addressed to you. And even more important are these words: "And I did not know him."

He says it twice. John the Baptist was a saint. He was the cousin of the Lord. For thirty years he lived in more or less close relations with Him and at the end of those thirty years he still didn't know Him! The Lord can have lived next to you since the beginning of your life and it is by no means certain that you would know him by a living faith in your hearts. You are no better than those people. Thirty years! And John the Baptist was a saint! And they were relatives! (Though relatives are often the people one notices least.)

Jesus had been foretold by the Prophets and the Patriarchs, he had been prefigured by all the just who suffered in the Old Testament. The contemporaries of Jesus were convinced that God would manifest himself by temporal retribution, rewarding the good and punishing the wicked. For them the most prosperous person was the most just, and the most miserably poor the worst sinner. For a long time mankind thought that suffering and sickness were signs of evildoing. A savage and naive attitude, which is still not entirely dead, led people to believe that God rewards the good and punishes the wicked here on earth. And so the unfortunate were considered to be guilty. It was a case where troubles never arrived singly. As soon as something unfortunate happened to you everyone immediately suspected that it was the result of some sin, and your friends got together and very kindly sounded out your conscience to reveal to you the sin which was the cause of your misfortune. Is that sort of thing so completely unknown to us today?

And even setting aside the Pharisees who pry into other people's consciences, doesn't it often happen to us that after some failure or accident, we feel vaguely guilty? We examine our consciences and ask ourselves what we could have done wrong to be punished like that. That is one of the most distressing things that I have encountered among people who are suffering; they could have endured their sickness if the best part of their strength had not been eaten away by this anxious self-interrogation, this fear that they are guilty and deserve to be humbled and made to suffer. When something bad happens to you, isn't your first reaction to say: "But what have I done to God?" We have the strength to endure misfortune, but not to endure the sense of guilt that then insinuates itself.

For centuries God has struggled against this seemingly ineradicable prejudice which makes us identify suffering with sin. From the beginning of the revelation God has shown us examples of just men suffering: Abel killed in a sacrifice, Joseph delivered into bondage, Isaac carrying the wood to his own funeral fire, Job innocent but attacked by his brothers. And God showed us those examples in order to prepare us to recognize and venerate the most Just, the most Suffering, the spotless Lamb of God who bears the sins of the world.

The prophets had foretold Christ, yet no one recognized him. So many ceremonies, so many chants among the Jews, so many liturgies, so many feasts in his honor. He was there — and no one recognized him. And if we had been near the Lord we would not have recognized him either. "To begin with I can rule out my brother, my sister, my husband, my wife, and then I can start looking for the Lord. . . ." Yes, but by then you will have already passed Him by. Those people believed in their priests, their relatives, their religion; but they didn't believe in God. God was in the midst of them and they didn't know him. It was prophetic. It happened with people who were no worse than you. They didn't know what they were doing, but they were doing it in good faith. When St. Paul persecuted Christ he did it out of ignorance. Jesus could have lived right next door to you since the beginning of your life and you wouldn't have noticed him. You would have stayed behind with those people who say, "We know all that." You would not have accepted Him, you would not have had that movement of living faith. The best would have followed him and imitated him before your eyes, but you would have remained unaware of his presence and his love.

When the Lord revealed himself to John the Baptist, John realized that he had never known him; and in that he was the precursor of our astonishing imperviousness to what is divine, to whatever is beyond us. "And I did not know him. But he who sent me to baptize with water said to me, 'He upon whom thou wilt see the Spirit descending, and abiding upon him, he it is who baptizes with the Holy Spirit."

It was at the moment of God's revelation that John realized that he was a sinner. And the more he realized that he was weak and feeble, the more God revealed himself as generous and giving. John the Baptist had the revelation of the Holy Trinity. He was the first to have that revelation. He knew everything at the moment that he realized that he knew nothing. He knew the most intimate secrets of the heart of Jesus. In that prodigious realization of his personal nothingness, he learned everything.

And there is an even more important lesson to be drawn from this, which is that one can never stop learning. One must discover for oneself what one has preached to others.

"Repent. Do penance. You are sinners." That is how the preaching of Jesus, of St. Peter, St. Paul and all the Apostles begins. John the Baptist preached the same thing to everyone, and then the day came when he learned that he had to begin with himself. "He must increase, but I must decrease." Jesus is going to grow and John the Baptist to diminish.

At the moment when Jesus is beginning to draw large crowds to himself, John the Baptist is in prison under squalid circumstances and not for the great cause of the Kingdom of God. He is threatened with death as a result of palace intrigues and thwarted lust. He is in prison, but he finds out what is going on.

John, too, had his ideas about the Kingdom of God. He had announced a Master who was going to put everyone in his place, who was going to punish the wicked and exalt the just. So he listened, and he was utterly disconcerted when he learned what the Lord was doing, that He was all Goodness, all Gentleness, that He was preaching love, forgiveness and poverty.

John felt at a loss. And there was also his personal situation. He had thought that the Lord would use His power to deliver him from prison. He thought that he had a talent to put at God's service and that he would be one of the Lord's lieutenants. But now that everything was beginning, he found himself in prison. So he waited for Jesus to come and deliver him; he believed, as we do, that the Redemption was going to begin with himself. But the days went by and he still wasn't set free. He sent his representatives to the Master: "Art thou he who is to come, or shall we look for another?" That is one of the most revealing passages in the Gospel.

We are all in a prison: our families, our

bad health, our weakness of character, our poverty, our jobs. And the things that we are expecting from the Lord, as a sign of his grace, is that he should deliver us from our prisons. "That is how he ought to come!"

Jesus sent this answer to John: "The blind see, the lame walk, the lepers are cleansed, the deaf hear, the dead rise, the poor have the gospel preached to them. And blessed is he who is not scandalized in me."

And then John understood the manner in which Jesus had come. You, too, will go through all the states of soul that he went through. John understood that he would not be delivered from prison. It took him some time, but at last he understood the prophecy, the Word of God, the way in which he, too, was working for the Kingdom of God. He accepted the manner in which the Lord had come. For while he remained in prison, by the strength of his faith and the force of his fidelity the deaf were beginning to hear, the blind to see, the lame to walk . . . and the poor were having the gospel preached to them. For what the Lord was sending him was a motive for remaining in prison forever.

We are all capable of remaining in prison

if we believe that doing so can serve some purpose.

You can all endure the suffering in your life if you know that it serves some good purpose. This is the message that the Lord sent to John, and John accepted it. He was willing and happy to remain where he was since around him there were lame people who could now walk, deaf people who could now hear and poor people who were being evangelized. He died content, and he, who in his childhood had learned to leap for joy in the presence of his Redeemer, learned at the end of his life to rejoice in pain and sorrow at the manner in which the Redemption was being carried out. He applied to himself everything that he had preached.

You must re-learn when old all that you knew when young. The older you grow the more you realize that you are a sinner. John learned to do himself all that he had taught others to do.

We are all scandalized by the manner in which the Lord comes into our lives. The Cross scandalized everybody. You must accept being scandalized or else you will be one of those charming but superficial Christians. Go step by step. Perhaps you will stumble, but never mind for that will teach you to step more surely. "And he, Son though he was, learned obedience from the things that he suffered."

In theory we are all ready to accept the cross. In practice it is always the wrong cross that is sent us. We will accept any cross other than the one that we actually have to bear. "This cross is embittering me. I have become a worse person since I have had to carry it. I thought that the cross was going to make me better, but in fact it's doing me harm, it's diminishing me."

But if the cross were to do us good, then perhaps it would not be a cross. For the cross is something that makes you suffer, that makes you fall, that diminishes you and restricts your apostolate. We are never in agreement with the way God treats us. But if we do not accept that cross, then we will never accept any cross.

St. John's death preceded the Passion of his Master. He was the Prophet and the Precursor of Him who, wishing to save the world, did not choose to save even himself but remained faithful even in the prison of his own Cross.

Through all our perplexity and doubt we will perhaps one day, like St. John the Baptist, be able to accept remaining in our prisons if we know that from that moment on, because of our sacrifice, the deaf will hear, the lepers be cleansed and the poor have the gospel preached to them.

Dialogue on Death
and Eternal Life

In the nineteenth century it was said that Christians resigned themselves to the evils of their day in the hope of a future life. They were congratulated on their good luck in being able to believe. People claimed to envy them because "their faith was such a consolation." From there it was but a short step to accuse them of believing in order to reassure themselves, from motives of self-interest or fear.

To this the Christians flung back the easy answer that if their opponents denied the after-life, it was because they were afraid of the punishments they might receive there!

Today such arguments are a thing of the past. Christians and unbelievers no longer argue about the future life but about the present one.

To be sure, Christians still claim to believe in "the resurrection of the body and the life everlasting." But they do so with such a lack of interest that it's almost as if they didn't believe in it. Certainly they don't appear to think about it very much.

But rather than question their faith in the resurrection it would be better to begin by discussing their *desire* for it.

Who wants to live forever? Who finds life so wonderful that he would want it to go on forever? Is there anything in your life that you would want to be made eternal?

Among the people you meet — the busy, the indifferent and the anxious — do you know any who give the impression that they would like things to go on as they are forever?

As for those who live a life of "pleasure," do you think they would want to be condemned to perpetual and forced pleasure? How much better even forced labor would be!

How can one preach resurrection to eternal life to people who no longer value life itself? Faith in resurrection can spring only from a great and living love. People in love promise to love one another forever, and a true love will not settle for anything less.

Our faith, our hope of resurrection for ourselves and for others depends strictly on our capacity for love. What is there that we love enough to make us want it eternalized, and ourselves with it? In other words, is there a person, a cause, a state of soul that you value so highly that you would want to make it part of your eternity? And is there a person you love enough to want to be eternal because of him?

Our capacity for redemption and resurrection, for ourselves and for others, may be gauged by the strength of our love.

Modern Christians are above all men of their times. And for a modern man it is infinitely more simple, more restful, more "consoling" to believe in annihilation (if he is merely tired) or (if he has a certain nobility) in a vague, unconscious survival either through his children or through humanity, whose lot he will have improved as a result of his labors.

Modern man is not greatly attached to himself; nor is he greatly attached to life. For him immortality is a threat and a burden rather than a promise or a consolation.

Faith in everlasting life is terribly disturbing, not only because of the threat of eternal punishments but quite simply because men are exhausted and have lost their taste for living. The thought of eternal life appalls them. How are they going to fill it? What have they experienced that they would like to see prolonged indefinitely? Is there anyone who finds his life so good that he would like it to go on forever?

"For my part," someone will say, "I have no desire for personal immortality. I don't attach such importance to my individual self that I would want to keep it forever. I'm satisfied with the thought that something of me will survive in my children. I need no future other than theirs, and I feel happy at the thought that, mingled with them, I will have a part in their discoveries, experiences, sufferings and joys. That is the only eternity that I need."

"But," one can reply, "if this fragment of yourself which continues to exist in your children has no self-awareness, no individual consciousness, it will be exactly the same as if there were nothing of you in your children. You yourself will have no part in their lives. The thought of doing so is enough to satisfy you so long as you can think (though you are not thinking very deeply); but what is death if not the extinction of the ability to think? That fragment of yourself which you like to think of as continuing to exist in your children will be no different from the steak and beans they had for dinner. What you are saying implies a denial of the capacity for conscious thought which distinguishes human nature from animal or vegetable nature. If carried to its logical conclusion, your argument would lead to canibalism. For if instead of eating meat and vegetables we were to eat people, we would then (according to your principles) insure their after-life."

"Very well then," the person will say. "Let us abandon this personal and individual form of immortality. But why not be satisfied with a continuation of life in humanity — a life which will be better and happier thanks to the efforts that we will have made? The human race forms a unity, and is evidently destined to unify itself even more. I make no distinction between my own destiny and the destiny of the human race. I feel that I am part of it and hope only for this form of eternal life."

"But the same answer applies to this new ambition," one can reply. "Of what use to man is membership in the human race if he cannot be conscious of it? He can take satisfaction in it now because he is conscious of it, but what will remain of that membership, and therefore of him, when he is no longer there to be conscious of it?

"Moreover, if human life ends with death, then our moral system must be reorganized on a new basis. Hitherto, by a strange phenomenon, mankind has 'always acted as if there were something more valuable than human life' (Saint-Exupéry). 'Nothing is worth turning away from one's love for,' said Camus. 'And yet it is impossible to accept being happy alone.'

"But if there is no after-life then we must get rid of these 'instinctive' ways of behaving. If everything comes to an end with death, then nothing can be more valuable than our own existence — certainly not the existence of others. We have a duty to ourselves to enjoy life and preserve it. To be sure we will practice a certain amount of generosity but only in so far as it will help our own self-development; certainly we will never go so far as to sacrifice ourselves without hope of reward.

"You say that you cannot live as a slave? But if you cease to be, you also cease to be free.

"You think that by refusing to live as a

slave you will be acting nobly? But if you lose your life you will also lose the nobility that you will have won by your sacrifice.

"You say that you are ready to give your life for those around you? But though you may leave them an example or an achievement, you will also at the same time be destroying the supreme value that you constitute for them: yourself. Nothing that you can give them can be more valuable than yourself. The best thing that you possess, your individual personality, cannot be transmitted.

"You say that you are willing to accept death in time of war to defend your wife and children? But surely you know that the greatest service you can render them is to keep yourself alive for their sake, even if your country has been occupied and enslaved.

"But no, you will give your life for your own sake, because you cannot tolerate slavery and injustice; and you will even sacrifice your home along with your life, so great is your faith in a higher value and a higher justice."

"But this higher value," the person will say, "is future society. It is the human race constantly elevating itself thanks to the self-sacrifice of its predecessors."

"That's splendid! Die on the battlefields so that the crops will grow better! Come now, think again, get rid of your false ideas and try and take a longer view. This human race of the future will one day perish. Neither mankind nor the world has any guarantee of eternity. You deny the after-life of the individual, so don't start deluding yourself by inventing a collective after-life. And anyway it's as pointless to want to prolong the life of the human race as it is to want to prolong the life of the individual. This great collective after-life is nothing more than a great collective agony. Humanity is not worth any more than an individual, nor is it any the less perishable.

"What must come to an end one day can perfectly well come to an end at once. It will make no difference to the galaxies whether the human race existed or did not exist, whether its existence was long or short, happy or unhappy.

"Moreover, you ought to have pity on your descendants and spare them the burden of your sacrifices. For what will be the most terrible thought in the minds of the last men on earth who witness the death of our planet? Precisely the thought of all the sacrifices whereby their predecessors ruined their own chances of happiness and spent their lives trying so vainly to prolong and improve the happiness and lives of their descendants.

"And again it is not, as you think, future society that is the object of your unselfish devotion; rather it is the values of generosity, truth and justice that you affirm by sacrificing yourself. This is so true that if present society stopped respecting and living by these values you would disassociate yourself from it; you would defend the individual who had been wronged against society, and you would rather that society perish than that it should triumph in injustice."

What positive proof is there of the immortality of the soul or the resurrection of the body? After all, nobody has ever returned from the beyond.

But yes, Christ rose from the dead. He showed himself living to his contemporaries, who have given their testimony. And he is still showing himself today, to us who are also his contemporaries, living in the lives and in the charity of true Christians. He has raised for himself a Body which can still be seen, heard and touched.

For resurrection is an immediate experience, an experience of the here and now.

Many Christians confuse the resurrection of the flesh with the resurrection of the body and therefore, of necessity, locate it far off in an indefinite future.

But the resurrection of the flesh is the resurrection of the whole man, and should not be confused with the resurrection of — meat! The Biblical meaning of the word "flesh" is "man," taken in the sense of his natural weakness. The soul is as much "flesh" as is the body. When you say that the Word was made flesh you are saying that it was made man. You would be heretical if you were to suppose that the Word took only a body!

How wretched is the situation of the Christian who on the one hand admits the immortality of the soul and on the other thinks that the great aim of Christ's ministry and the Redemption is to insure that after hundreds of years have gone by, mere meat will be resurrected! After centuries of doing very well without them and of living as "separated souls," we will get our bodies back — rather as if they were superfluous but decorative appendages.

Most Christians believe in the resurrection of the flesh in the way that Martha did. When Christ said to her, "Thy brother shall rise," Martha replied: "I know that he will rise at the resurrection, on the last day." It was so far off that she wasn't interested. She was about as enthusiastic as Catholics who declare: "I am awaiting the resurrection of the dead."

But Christ was speaking of another resurrection, of a resurrection that was immediate. "I am the Resurrection and the Life; he who believes in me, even if he die, shall live." This is something quite different.

All Christian life is a succession of experiences of death and resurrection. It begins with baptism. "We were buried with him by means of baptism into his death" and we have come out transformed, brought to life, made immortal. All the sacraments are participations in the death and resurrection of Christ. But have you ever really and truly *experienced* such a transformation?

There are two signs by which you may know that you have been resurrected.

The first is the realization that you have been dead. So long as you are dead, you cannot realize it; you don't suffer, you don't feel bad, you don't feel anything. It is only when you come to life again that you suddenly realize that you have been dead, and how long and how greatly. You are bewildered and ask yourself: "How could I have endured that for such a long time? I believed in nothing, expected nothing, hoped for nothing, I loved nothing and no one; and I felt perfectly all right and had nothing to say at confession. I was dead!"

It's like being in a room where all the windows and doors are closed. The people in it gradually asphyxiate and lose consciousness; they feel warm and doze off. But when someone throws open a window and the fresh air comes rushing in, then they wake up, bestir themselves, notice the stench and ask themselves: "How on earth could we have stayed in a place smelling like that?"

The sign that you have been resurrected is the realization that you have been dead. The sign that you are beginning to see is when you say to yourself: "How could I have been so blind?" The sign that you are beginning to hear is when you say to yourself: "I have been told for years but this is the first time that I have understood it." The man who was born blind in the Gospel is us. The deaf-mute in the Gospel is us. And the resurrection that Christ promises is ours.

Moreover, the life into which we are resurrected by Christ is the eternal life, a life which can last forever. From the moment of resurrection the life into which we awake is one of peace, joy, love and an abundance of life and faith which we could live on forever. We are launched into an infinite life. We could both die at once and live forever.

We discover that there are two kinds of life in us: a poor, miserable, sad little life, bored and boring, and God grant that that sort of life should not go on forever! And there is another life so intense and enjoyable that not even eternity can exhaust it.

It is then that we understand the words of Christ: "This is the bread that comes down from heaven, so that if anyone eat of it he will not die." There is in us a life that will never end. "He who eats my flesh and drinks my blood has life everlasting . . . This is the bread that has come down from heaven; not as your fathers ate the manna, and died. He who eats this bread shall live forever." And "Whoever lives and believes in me shall not die . . . Amen, amen, I say to you, if anyone keeps my word, he will never see death."

And He asks us: "Dost thou believe this?"

For a long time I understood the words of St. Peter to Christ: "Lord, to whom shall we go? Thou hast the words of everlasting life," as an act of faith, a gesture of trust. But now I see them as expressing above all an experience: "Nobody has spoken to us like you. You are telling us the truth of things and of life. You speak of what is innermost in us with an authority, as of something that you have experienced yourself. You have revealed in us a life that we did not know existed. We can never tire of hearing you, and when you speak we know that you are opening the gates of true life."

How can someone who has not experienced resurrection and immortal life here on earth really believe in them for the hereafter?

All faith depends on experience. Because He has already resurrected me once, I have the right to believe that He will resurrect me again. And I have some good news, a "Gospel," to announce to the world: "If He can resurrect a poor wretch like me, then He can resurrect everyone else. I am the bearer throughout the world of an extraordinary offer of life and resurrection."

If men are not raised from the dead, then neither did Christ rise from the dead! This is a daring formulation of of our faith, one which may have escaped even St. Paul, but true nonetheless.

Let us not try to pacify the anguish and re-

volt of mankind with promises of the hereafter. Instead let us announce the good
news, the revolutionary and joyful news:
men can live, liberate themselves, be resurrected and know another kind of life here
on earth.

And let us invite everyone to verify Christ's
resurrection by undergoing the experience
of his own resurrection!

But what about those who find this faith
too sublime?

Let me cite another personal experience.
I have seen men die for a cause. They were
radiant with life and joy. They knew with absolute certainty that their bodies had nothing
to do with their real selves, that their earthly life was without importance when set
against the one they were living, which was
invulnerable to bullets and blows. They were
experiencing the prodigious reality of spiritual life. They were living in it at that moment and forever.

Many of them undoubtedly had no ex-
plicit thoughts of an after-life. All they felt
was that no matter what might happen they
were doing the right thing; if need be, they
would do it again. They had reached a state
where regret was impossible.

With a humility that was much more true

and moving than that of those who are re-signed to total disappearance after death, they were not thinking of their future life. But if they had been asked, they woud have affirmed without the slightest shadow of doubt the value of what they were doing.

They were not asking for a reward; they were devoting themselves so passionately to the cause they were serving that they no longer thought of themselves as separate from it. They had identified themselves with it so completely that they would have been incapable of denying it and affirming them-selves. The nature of the spiritual life they were living at those moments appeared to them so clearly that they could no longer think of themselves as mortal.

It was not from fear, nor from self-interest, but solely from love that they knew them-selves to be immortal. They had found some-thing of such great value that they wanted to live, wanted to know that they were living, for it.

There is no immortality for the person who does not love life.

There is no resurrection for the person who has found nothing to love.

Only love knows that it will love forever.

But is there no proof of a more strictly philosophical nature of the immortality of the soul?

The proof that has just been given is perfectly philosophical, and you may distrust it only because of its emotional context. Yet there is another proof, one from awareness of our spirituality which can demonstrate the immortality of the soul.

It is to be noted that the immortality of the soul cannot be "proved," in the proper sense of the term, any more than we can prove absolute immateriality. One can only prove that the soul is not material, and therefore not decomposable, and therefore not mortal.

What is matter and what are its characteristics? Evidently it has nothing to do with taste, touch, visibility and so on, for thanks to our scientific instruments we know that only a very small part of the material world is accessible to our senses.

The most precise definition of matter is this: matter is something which exists in time and in space; something which at a given moment can be in only one place; something which exists only at a single moment in time and at a single point in space.

Now there exist in us activities which are

outside time and space. Mental awareness is outside space; I am aware that I know, I am aware that I am aware. This doubling back, this dual vision is impossible in the material order. To be able to distinguish oneself from oneself to the point where one can consider oneself as a separate object and yet still be with oneself is a faculty that lies outside the material order. We are at one and the same time the subject and the object of our cognition. If we were only the subject, we would know the rest without knowing ourselves; but then we would not know that we know, we would be unaware of our knowing and so we would not even be subjects of cognition. For in order to be the subject we must be both our own subject and object. Material activity is clearly incapable of that. As someone once said: "The action of knitting can be applied to wool or cotton, and scarves can be made out of them; but the action of knitting cannot be applied to the action of knitting."

Moreover, our mental activity is outside time

An experience common to everyone will clarify the spiritual nature of our thought processes. When I hear a sentence, I cannot understand it properly until it has been com-

pleted. This means that in my inner time sequence I am preserving in a state of simul-
taneity all the words of the sentence which
were spoken one after the other in their external time sequence. And this in turn means
that there is something in me which is outside time, and which alone allows us to understand something that exists in time.

If I existed only in the external time sequence, I would be able to connect only
with each separate word (or only with each
syllable or each letter) and I wouldn't even
know that there had been a succession of
words; for to know that there has been a
succession of words I have to be able to re-
hear the words that have been spoken while
at the same time listening to the word that is
being spoken. "But," someone will say, "I
am keeping the words in my memory." Yes,
but if your memory is material then it should
keep them and reproduce them as they were
spoken, that is to say in sequence; whereas
to understand the whole sentence the words
must be reproduced simultaneously.

So if I understand the sentence it is because at one and the same time I am aware
of the passage of time (i.e., the succession of
words) and I also escape the passage of time,
at least partially, by means of that part of

myself which is aware of the succession.

Thus there exists in us a timeless present into which we gather all the elements that have occurred successively in time. We are present at a progressive unfolding but without fully taking part in it; we are in time since we are subject to its action, and outside time since we can make the results of that action simultaneous. For us the present and the past are equally present; in other words we are outside time.

We are capable of transcending time and seeing its results in one single, simultaneous ensemble.

Basically the spiritual life, if it were entirely recollected and true to itself, would keep gathered together permanently in its interior present all the conscious moments of its existence. Its only awareness of death would be that its enrichment had come to an end . . . or by the beginning of another mode of cognition. Its eternity would consist of all the moments when it was alive during its temporal existence. And that is enough to fill a heaven or a hell.

So there you have two proofs: that of the experience of death and that of our mental activity, and they both come to the same thing. They make us aware of the fact that we exist in time, and yet outside time; in this world, and yet not of this world. We are involved in a temporal development from which a whole part of ourselves is already emerging.

DATE DUE
